Climate Crisis: Alarmists Vs. Deniers

Richard G. Kaye

Richard Gregory Kaye KRG Publishing 11498 68th St. Largo, Florida 33773

kevinrgiven@gmail.com

Cover Pixabay.

Photos: Markus Spiske, Vincent M. A. Jansen, Saph Photography, Harrison Haines, Kira Schwarz, Vlad Chetan, Asad, Oliver Sjöström, Symeon Ekizoglou, Magda Ehlers, Josh Hild, Matthew T. Rader, Ralph W. Lambrecht

Table of Contents

Forward

I am not a scientist. Although I have a basic High School education in the subject, I took no science courses in college. Therefore, I could not argue about any formula in this volume.

So, why am I authoring a book on a very scientific subject? I believe it is not only possible but essential to discuss this topic from the position of a layman. Can we decipher what the big brains are saying and understand what is going on with climate? I firmly believe we can, and I'm here to guide you through it.

I may not know as much about the scientific method as many of those I discuss in this volume, but I do know patterns and B.S., to put it politely as I can. We can look at the claims of those who know the scientific method, see if they can be corroborated historically, and see what the historical record tells us.

I invite you to join me on this quest to learn precisely what the "experts" say about climate and crisis. What they've said historically and what they are saying today.

Richard

1

An Observation

Look for Kevin Given's Video About This Book on YouTube!

"The Science is settled!" Have you ever heard that statement? It is made when people do not want an open-minded discussion on a scientific topic. But how can science be settled when the premise of scientific knowledge is experimenting and testing what we know to be true? At one time, scientific thought taught us that the world was flat and perched upon the back of a turtle (1). At another time, it was taught that the universe had no beginning but always existed (2). These thoughts have been challenged by what we have discovered and tested through the scientific method. Science is never "settled". It is tentative.

Definition of science:

1: the state of knowing: knowledge as distinguished from ignorance or misunderstanding

2:

a: a department of systematized knowledge as an <u>object of study</u> in the science of theology

b: something (such as a sport or technique) that may be <u>studied or learned,</u> like systematized knowledge.

have it down to a science

3:

a: knowledge or a system of knowledge covering general truths or the <u>operation of general laws</u>, especially as obtained and tested through scientific methods<u>.</u>

b: such knowledge or such a system of knowledge <u>concerned with the physical world and its phenomena</u>: natural science.

4:

A system or method reconciling <u>practical ends with scientific laws,</u> cooking is both a science and an art.

(emphasis mine)

When we learn something that we always thought was true does not always adhere to the facts, we must change our thinking on a particular topic. The alarmists and the deniers must accept the facts based on scientific research and the historical record.

Whose ideas can be verified through research, the alarmists or the deniers? Both make good points and sometimes sound plausible, but what about the historical record? Whose ideas match what has already gone on? Is the Greenhouse effect a fact or a theory? Before we look at that, we must define the greenhouse effect.

From Merriam-Webster:

Definition of the greenhouse effect

Warming of the surface and lower atmosphere of a planet (such as Earth or Venus) caused by the conversion of solar radiation into heat in a process involving the selective transmission of short-wave solar radiation by the atmosphere, its absorption by the planet's surface, and reradiation as infrared, which is absorbed and partly reradiated back to the surface by atmospheric gases.

We are supposed to believe that atmospheric gases are partly responsible for the warming of the surface of planet Earth. The alarmists would have us believe that humankind is either partly or wholly responsible for the surface warming due to the amount of CO_2 absorbed into our world's atmosphere.

But does this hold historically? Does co-relation lead to causation? Humankind has put little CO_2 into the atmosphere compared to what nature herself has dispersed into the air—only about 0.04% (3).

Is this enough to generate all the panic the Climate crisis alarmists are trying to cause? Are the Climate crisis deniers wrong to say there is nothing to worry about? Let's look at the historical record.

During the 1920s and 1930s, the temperature got hot. The winter of 1936 was one of the coldest on record, while the summer of that year was one of the hottest. (4) The Dust Bowl was used to describe this era as the topsoil in the Midwest was scorched, and the slightest wind could cause massive dust storms. The Dust Bowl era peaked in 1935. In addition to the astronomically elevated temperatures, farmers contributed to the catastrophe with improper knowledge of their equipment and techniques (5).

What caused this incredible heat in the 1920s and 30s? I don't know, but one thing I do know is that it had nothing to do with C02 emissions. The C02 emitted into the atmosphere was about on par with the industrial age, and humankind had little to do with it. Gasoline-powered vehicles had barely come on the market, and commercial airlines had not yet materialized.

Let's look at some headlines from the 1930s to see how bad the crisis was:

"Great Dust Cloud Drifts from Western States to East" – Pittston Gazette May 11 -1934

"Dust Storm Obscures Chicago Skyscrapers" – The Waco News-Tribune May 14–1934

"Boy, 7, Found Suffocated in Kansas Dust Storm" – Oakland Tribune March 17-1935

"Denton in Grip of Worst Dust Storm Ever Seen Here" – Denton Record-Chronicle April 11, 1935

"Oklahoma Families Flee Dust" – Arizona Republic April 11, 1935

"United Press Writer Tells a Vivid Story of Dust Storm Area" – April 16, 1935

"Farmers Fear Judgment Day in Dust Storm" – Pittsburgh Press April 17, 1935

"Estimate Crop Damages in Dust Storm Area $30,000,000; Farmers Hope for Rain" – The News Chronicle April 19, 1935

"Dust Turns Day into Night, Closes Schools, Blocks Roads" – Cincinnati Enquirer February 18, 1937

"Fugitives from Dust Bowls Find Meager Living on Coast" – Tampa Daily News June 7, 1938

"Workers from Dust Bowl Provide Problem in Relief in California" – Oakland Tribune April 8, 1938

As the years went on, the temperature began to level off in the late 1940s and 1950s and then became freezing during the 1960s and 1970s, leading the Climate crisis alarmists of that age to warn mankind of a phenomenon known as Global Cooling. (6) Look at what the "experts" said during the 1970s.

<u>1970 – New Ice Age May Descend on Man</u>.

Should a new ice age descend upon the earth in the centuries immediately ahead, man – or at least those yet unasphyxiated survivors from his present billions – may have to acknowledge that he brought it on himself.

That, at least, would seem to be the latest horror story from the pollution front. Since the advent of the Industrial Revolution, debris from manufacturing processes has accumulated in the atmosphere to such an extent that the earth is now enveloped in a layer of dust, reflecting into space a portion of the energy radiated from the sun. (7)

Pollution Could Cause Ice Age, Agency Reports.

Continued pollution of the atmosphere with smoke, dust, and other small particles "may ultimately create eternal winter on earth." A government agency said yesterday. quoting Dr. Earl W Barret of the ESSA Laboratories, Boulder, Colorado. (8)

Another Ice Age? Pollution Blocking Sunlight.

Air pollution may cause another ice age, according to a Japanese meteorologist, **Dr. Tadashi Yano**. He says that in the last 30 years, waste particles in the atmosphere have already blocked enough sunlight to cause the average world temperature to drop nearly one degree. (9)

New Evidence Indicates Ice Age Here.

Weather satellites sweeping across the Northern Hemisphere have come up with a surprise: The permanent snow and ice cap has increased sharply.

A recently completed study of weekly maps of the National Oceanic and Atmospheric Administration states that the snow and ice increased by 12 percent in the Northern Hemisphere in 1971 and has remained at a new level.

The study was done by George and Helen Kukla of the Lamont Doherty Geological Observatory of Columbia University. (10)

International Team of Specialists Finds No End in Sight to 30-Year Cooling Trend in Northern Hemisphere.

Based on eight climate indexes, an international team of specialists has concluded that the cooling trend of the last 30 years, at least in the Northern Hemisphere, is not ending.

In some, but not all, cases, the data extended through last winter. They include sea surface temperatures in the northcentral Pacific and North Atlantic, air temperatures at the surface and various elevations, and the extent of snow and ice cover at different seasons.

In all cases, it has been found that the year-to-year variations in climate are far more marked than the long-term trend. The long-term trend often becomes evident only when data from several years are displayed.

The report, prepared by German, Japanese, and American specialists, appears in the Dec. 15 issue of Nature, the British journal. The findings indicate that from 1950 to 1975, the cooling per decade of most climate indexes in the Northern Hemisphere was from 0.1 to 0.2 degrees Celsius, 0.2 to 0.4 degrees Fahrenheit. (11)

Many more articles from the 1970s discuss how pollution particles prevent a certain amount of sunlight from entering our atmosphere. Carbon emissions cause sunlight to be reradiated back to the surface.

But something doesn't quite add up here. The 1970s should have toasted us if the greenhouse effect were actual. The amount of carbon that man was putting into the atmosphere, as we can see by the chart at the beginning of this chapter, increased tenfold. So how come it got colder? The "experts" of the seventies warned us of a coming ice age and that we could be frozen within a few years.

Leonard Nimoy (Mr. Spock from *Star Trek*) hosted the program In *Search Of Season* Two, episode 23 (of 47 total episodes) dedicated an entire episode to *The Coming Ice Age*.

Here's my observation and review of that episode.

So, what information did Nimoy present about Global Cooling, and did it happen? You can find the show on YouTube for further viewing. Before we go into what that program is given, we'll read the disclaimer at the beginning of each episode: *This series presents information based on theory and conjecture. The producer aims to suggest some explanations for the mysteries we will examine, but not necessarily the only ones.*

This episode begins with a man walking along the road in a cold blizzard, and Nimoy's narration tells us, "In 1977, the worst winter in a century struck the United States."

The show goes on to inform us that the weather was so bad that it stopped traffic in Buffalo, New York, and eight people froze to death in their cars. Then, Pat Bushnell reflects on her experience being stuck on the road that night.

Then Nimoy informs us that the brutal Buffalo winter might become common throughout the United States. He states that climate "experts" believe that the next ice age is on its way, and according to recent evidence, it could come sooner than expected. The discussion then switches to nature's violent tendencies and storms threatening the planet.

After that, Nimoy discusses how the recent (in terms of earth's age) comfortable cycle of spring sowing, summer growth, and fall harvest is abnormal in terms of long history. Only in the last ten thousand years has Earth enjoyed continuous warmth. For millions of years, the earth was covered in ice. Then he explains that all that is left of the great glaciers that covered North America are the ice caps of the Canadian Arctic. If the ice spreads over the continent again, the process will begin on Baffin Island in northern Canada.

This is where the narration tells us that we will look for clues about the coming ice age. He tells us that the last ice age was 115 thousand years ago, as animation shows ice covering the continent. Then he describes how the ice retreated until we enjoyed a warming period, which allowed us to flourish and see population growth of 5 billion people worldwide (remember this was in 1977).

Nimoy asks when the abnormal warmth will end, and the next ice age will begin. Then we cut to Dr. Gifford Miller, a glaciologist who claims that the warm period ended on Baffin Island 3,000 years ago! (Emphasis mine.) He tells us that the glaciers have expanded since then. He also tells us that the summer of 1972 was one of the most severe on record, and the ice on Baffin Island did not retreat that year.

Residents discuss how the summers of the recent decade have not seen the ice diminish at all. The narrator states that at the rate the temperatures have dropped over the last thirty years, we could see ice age conditions within the next two hundred years.

The sober reality, as presented by Nimoy, is that the result could be hunger and death on a scale unprecedented in all of history.

"The threat of an ice age is not as unprecedented as they once thought! During our grandchildren's lifetime, arctic cold and perpetual snow could turn most of the inhabitable forces of our planet into a polar desert."

The program then shows us research cutting up thousands of years-old ice and shipping it south to be studied. The scientists involved discovered that at a certain level, the ice froze "with dramatic suddenness."

The show cuts to a segment featuring Dr. Chester Langway, chair of the geology department at the State University of New York, Buffalo. He tells us that at one point 89,000 years ago, the earth was warm, and an event, volcanic activity, triggered the ice age.

We go on to follow the research ship Vemma as she takes samples of sediments. Geologists had taken enough samples to reveal a detailed history of climate. We're introduced to another climate "expert", Dr. James Hays. He has shown us that there have theoretically been eight ice ages in the last seven hundred thousand years. Hays claims that since we can show the ice ages of the past, we can predict when the next one will happen...and we are currently headed towards one! (Though none of the evidence corroborating this claim is shown or discussed.)

Then, we are treated to a montage of images from the winter of 1976-77 from Chicago, Dayton, Cincinnati, and more, detailing how cold it got. Then, we are back to Buffalo and Pat Bushnell's memory of that winter.

Nimoy then speculates what we can do to prevent the coming ice age. He suggests using nuclear power to loosen the polar ice caps. Another suggestion involves covering the poles with black soot to increase sunlight absorption.

Then we are back to another "expert," Dr. Stephen Schneider, a National Center for Atmospheric Research climatologist. We finally have an "expert" telling us what we should have known.

"Can we do these things? Yes. But will they make things better? I'm not sure. We can't predict with any certainty what's happening to our climactic future. How can we come along and intervene in that ignorance? You Could melt the ice caps. What would that do to the coastal cities? The cure could be worse than the disease. Would that be better or worse than the risk of an ice age?"

Then, we have some closing remarks from Mr. Nimoy. This episode is sobering in its bleak outlook and plays on the fears of its audience. However, extraordinarily little evidence supports the claims that we are headed into another ice age. We do see some of the research done to categorize how these experts come to their conclusions, which is fascinating. To the show's credit, the final "expert" tells us that we can't predict what will happen.

The show also doesn't tell us much about how man is responsible for any of this if mankind is somehow involved. There are only vague references to pollution, and I don't recall any mention of C02 during this episode.   With what happened in the coming decades, we can only thank God that none of the suggestions of covering the ice caps with soot or using nuclear power to melt them were tried.

In Conclusion, it is a very entertaining episode that doesn't entirely sell its concept. But what can you expect from a show that takes the Loch Ness Monster and the Abominable Snow Man seriously? The fact that its two narrators, Rod Serling and Leonard Nimoy, were stars of popular 1960s science fiction shows should tell you all you need to know about the accuracy of this series.

We went from scorching temperatures in the 1930s and 1940s to frigid temperatures in the 1970s. This is despite the advancing Industrial Age, which significantly increased mankind's pumping of C02 into the atmosphere. According to the Greenhouse effect, shouldn't we have been scorched to death?

Save our Planet

Naturland
ÖKOLOGISCH!
FOR FUTURE!

OUR PLANET
OUR FUTURE
THERE'S NO PLANET B

FIGHT
CLIMATE
CHANGE
OR
DIE
FRYING
DONT BE A
FOSSIL FOOL
ACT NOW

OUR PLANET
IS GETTING
HOTTER
THAN COLE
SPROUSE

You'll die of
OLD AGE
we'll die of
CLIMATE CHANGE

I WANT
A HOT
DATE NOT
A HOT
PLANET
phy
HANDLE WITH CARE
THIS WAY UP

2

Could Mr. Spock Be Wrong?

One of the first space shuttles was named after the Starship Enterprise on Star Trek.

It couldn't be! Not the first officer aboard the U.S.S. Enterprise. Say it isn't so. Captain Kirk only glances over at his first officer, who happens to be the science officer aboard the ship, to get a complete explanation of not just the science but also the history of whatever topic *Star Trek* is tackling that week.

Spock calculates everything down to the minute details and seems to have a computer for a brain. As ship surgeon Dr. Leonard McCoy points out from time to time. But of course, Mr. Spock is a fictional character played by actor Leonard Nimoy, who also hosted a show called *In Search of...*

It was a series with an episode called *The Coming Ice Age*. We examined that episode in the previous chapter, and one statement that stands out to me is from Mr. Nimoy: "During the lifetime of our grandchildren, arctic cold and perpetual snow could turn most of the inhabitable forces of our planet into a polar desert." It's essential to question this statement and think critically about its implications.

That statement was made in 1978, and Leonard Nimoy's grandchildren are young adults, and most of the inhabitable forces of our planet are not a polar desert.

Jonah Nimoy is Leonard Nimoy's youngest grandchild, and he's only about 11 years older than Greta Thunberg. The climate alarmists did not see their dire predictions happen. We will investigate Greta Thunberg and her significance in a later chapter, but the point I want to make in this chapter is that the *Global Cooling* activists of the 1970s did not see their dire predictions come to pass.

Let's look at more predictions:

"If man keeps piping pollution into the atmosphere, he could bring on a new ice age that would **cover states like Florida (where I live, incidentally) with 400 feet of water**" – Paul Cato (12) (emphasis mine)

The forty-six scientists who gathered at Brown University, Providence, R. I., for a symposium on "The End of the Present Interglacial" agreed that there is evidence of an ominous worldwide cooling of temperatures in the past two decades.

They also expressed fear that man, through air pollution, may be hastening the natural process. (13)

… long-range forecasts, at least from some sources, indicate that winters will gradually become colder. **Madeleine Briskin,** a geologist at the University of Cincinnati, says that we are entering a "Little Ice Age" and that our immediate future calls for more severe winters and cooler summers most years.

Although there's some disagreement about the causes of this cold trend, **there's widespread agreement among experts that it's happening**. (emphasis mine) (14)

Some specialists argue that a new ice age is on the horizon, either as a natural cyclical process or due to human-caused pollution of the atmosphere. Interestingly, some experts suggest that such pollution could prevent an ice age. This underscores the significant impact that human activity can have on the environment.

Eventually, a significant cooling of the climate is widely considered inevitable. Hints that it may already have begun are evident. The drop in mean temperatures since 1950 in the Northern Hemisphere has been sufficient, for example, to shorten Britain's growing season for crops by two weeks. (15)

There are ominous signs that the Earth's weather patterns have begun to change dramatically and that these changes may portend a drastic decline in food production – with profound political implications for about every nation on Earth. The drop in food output could begin quite soon, only ten years from now. The regions destined to feel its impact are the great wheat-producing lands of Canada and the U.S.S.R. in the North, along with several marginally self-sufficient tropical areas – parts of India, Pakistan, Bangladesh, Indochina, and Indonesia – where the growing season is dependent upon the rains brought by the monsoon.

The evidence supporting these predictions has accumulated so massively that meteorologists are hard-pressed to keep up with it. In England, farmers have seen their growing season decline by about two weeks since 1950, resulting in an overall loss in grain production estimated at up to 100,000 tons annually.

During the same time, the average temperature around the equator has risen by a fraction of a degree – a fraction that, in some areas, can mean drought and desolation. Last April, in the most devastating outbreak of tornadoes ever recorded, 148 twisters killed more than 300 people and caused half a billion dollars worth of damage in 13 U.S. states.

To scientists, these disparate incidents represent the advanced signs of fundamental changes in the world's weather. The central fact is that the earth's climate is cooling down after three-quarters of a century of extraordinarily mild conditions. **Meteorologists disagree about the cause and extent of the cooling trend and its impact on local weather conditions. However, they are almost unanimous in their view that the trend will reduce agricultural productivity for the rest of the century.** (emphasis mine) If the climatic change is as profound as some of the pessimist's fear, the resulting famines could be catastrophic. "A major climatic change would force economic and social adjustments on a worldwide scale," warns a recent report by the <u>National Academy of Sciences</u>, "because the global patterns of food production and population that have evolved are implicitly dependent on the climate of the present century." (16)

The Arctic ice and snow cap have expanded by 12 percent in the last decade, and for the first time this century, ships making for Iceland ports have been impeded by drifting ice.

...scientists also expressed concern over the increasing importance of man's effects on climate. **They said it is unclear whether the increased levels of carbon dioxide in the atmosphere, caused by burning fuel, will alter temperature.** (emphasis mine) (17)

"We are on a definite downhill course for the next two centuries," He (Prof. **Hubert Lamb,** director of climate research at the University of East Anglia) declared. "The last 20 years (1980-1999) of this century will be progressively colder. After that, **the climate may warm up again, but only for decades.**" This unpredictability of future climate trends underscores the need for preparedness and adaptation.

Many more in-depth articles appeared in the 1970's, some from scientific journals, and went into greater detail about what they believed was happening.

Growing up in the State of Maine, I remember the summer of 1977 or '78 at Houlton High School. It was in June. We looked out the window, and it started snowing. And I don't mean light dusting; it snowed for a few hours and stayed a few days. DURING THE MONTH OF JUNE! Yeah, the 1970s were one cold decade. It even snowed in Florida (Where I live now), which we had never seen before.

Wikipedia: January 18, 1977: The pressure gradient between a strong ridge over the Mississippi Valley and a Nor'easter over Atlantic Canada sends cold temperatures southward into the state. Areas around Pensacola are the first to receive snow, followed by the rest of the Panhandle. Following record accumulations for The Nature Coast, the I-4 corridor (both Orlando and Tampa) receives light accumulations of 0.2 inches (5.1 mm) to 0.5 inches (13 mm).

By early morning before sunrise on January 19, West Palm Beach reported snow flurries in the air for the first and only time on record, with snow flurries reaching as far south as Homestead. The snow caused little impact as it was of the dry variety, melting on contact and lasting less than 40 minutes. Cold air damages the winter citrus industry by hundreds of millions of dollars (Orlando tied the 1899 record of over six consecutive nights well below freezing).

On January 20, The Miami Herald reports the event as the front-page story, with a headline of a size usually reserved for the declaration of war (19)

What happened? We were supposed to see increasingly cold temperatures throughout the rest of the century. The experts have spoken. They're scientists, aren't they? Isn't "the science settled"? **Paul Cato, Madeleine Briskin, Hubert Lamb, The National Academy of Sciences, and a panel of 46 scientists at Brown University** preach doom and gloom for the near future. But, when we come to the 1980s, we don't see it getting colder; the opposite happened. The same experts preaching a global cooling trend in the 1960s and 1970s were now changing their tune and began preaching about global warming.

The consensus had changed. So, the science wasn't settled? The ice age isn't coming. What were the predictions about climate change during the 1980s?

NASA Scientist James Hanson is the father of the modern global warming movement. He testified before Congress, on a scorching day, June 23, 1988, to be precise, that "the greenhouse effect had been detected and is changing our climate now." (20)

June 11, 1986. A global warming trend could bring heat waves, dust-dry farmland, and disease, the experts said… Under this scenario, the resort town of Ocean City, Md., will lose 39 feet of shoreline by 2000 and 85 feet within the next 25 years. (21)

"If the current pace of the buildup of these gases continues, the effect is likely to be a warming of 3 to 9 degrees Fahrenheit [between now and] the year 2025 to 2050…. The rise in global temperature is predicted to … cause sea levels to rise by one to four feet by the middle of the next century." Philip Shabecoff. (22)

Coastal flooding and crop failures would create an exodus of "eco- refugees, threatening political chaos, said Noel Brown, director of the New York office of the U.N. Environment Program, or UNEP.

He said governments have a 10-year window of opportunity to solve the greenhouse effect before it goes beyond human control.

As the warming melts polar icecaps, ocean levels will rise by up to three feet... (23)

Sleds, snowmen, snowballs, and the excitement of waking to find that the stuff has settled outside are all a rapidly diminishing part of Britain's culture as warmer winters – which scientists are attributing to global climate change – produce not only fewer white Christmases but fewer white Januarys and Februarys...Global warming, the heating of the atmosphere by increased amounts of industrial gases, is now accepted as a reality by the international community...**within a few years, snowfall will become "a very rare and exciting event."** (emphasis mine) – Dr. David Viner (24)

Of all the possible ways climate change could affect our planet, this is the most bizarre: as the oceans warm up, Earth will rotate a little faster, reducing the length of a day.

Anything that changes the distribution of the planet's mass relative to its axis of rotation affects the time it takes for Earth to complete one rotation.

"Think of an ice skater who is spinning," says Felix Landerer of the Max Planck Institute for Meteorology in Hamburg, Germany. "When you stretch your arms out, you slow down, and when you bring your arms closer to your body, you spin faster." It seems Earth will hug itself slightly tighter because of global warming. (25)

Arctic Summers Ice Free 'By 2013'

Their latest modeling studies indicate that northern polar waters could be ice-free in summers within 5-6 years.

<u>**Professor Wieslaw Maslowski**</u> told an American Geophysical Union meeting that those previous projections underestimated the processes driving ice loss.

Summer melting this year reduced the ice cover to 4.13 million sq. km, the smallest ever.

Remarkably, this stunning low point was not even incorporated into **Professor Maslowski's** and his team's model runs, which used data sets from 1979 to 2004 in projections.

Using supercomputers to crunch through likely future outcomes has become a standard part of climate science. **Former US Vice President Al Gore cited Professor Maslowski's analysis on Monday in his acceptance speech at the Nobel Peace Prize ceremony in Oslo.** (emphasis mine) (26)

In chapter one, we saw failed predictions from global cooling alarmists. In this chapter, we touched on a few global warming alarmists. The experts were supposed to be correct, and the science is settled: anyone who is a climate crisis denier should be locked up and thrown away the key.

Now, many alarmists are claiming that anyone who disagrees with them is a racist. (27) Strong charges from groups like the Sierra Club. Why would you verbally attack someone you disagree with ad hominem? Those who cannot defend their position have to resort to name-calling.

I always thought a racist was someone who dislikes another person because of the color of their skin, not because they do not accept the arguments of the Crisis Alarmists. I will deal with these types in another chapter, but now I want to re-cap and move on.

The growth of carbon emissions during the industrial age, from the 'Dust Bowl' era of the 1930s, did not raise temperatures. Instead, temperatures leveled off in the 1940s and 1950s and then got cold during the 1960s and 1970s.

Leonard Nimoy's grandchildren don't live in a polar desert.

Florida and other coastal states aren't under 400 feet of water.

Food Production is up, not down.

Winters did not get colder in our 'immediate future' from the 1980s to the turn of the century.

During the coldest period of the 1970s, we saw snow in Florida, not just flurries.

Snowfall is not rare today.

Arctic summers did not become ice-free by 2017.

"Experts" like **Paul Cato, Madeleine Briskin, Hubert Lamb, Philip Shabecoff, Dr. David Viner, Felix Landerer, Noel Brown,** The National Academy of Sciences, and a panel of 46 scientists at Brown University were wrong with their predictions about climate.

No, Mr. Spock, the fictional character on *Star Trek,* is not wrong. However, the all-too-human actor who played him can be incorrect. He even authored a book on the topic called "I Am Not Spock" (Later on, he wrote another book called "I Am Spock")

Just because some of the climate crisis alarmists were wrong with some of their predictions doesn't necessarily mean that they were mistaken in the long run. But I want to devote the next chapter to one of their predictions...

Predictions about snowfall becoming rare and an ice-free arctic summer have not come to pass...yet!

How endangered are Polar Bears? Read on and find out!

FIGHT
CLIMATE
CHANGE
OR
DIE
FRYING
DONT BE A
FOSSIL FOOL
ACT NOW

ECONOT EGO

PLANET
over
PROFIT

OCEANS RISE
&
OVERFLOW
IT AIN'T RIGHT
&
IT AIN'T NATU
SEE HOW THE
COULD BE IN SPITE
OF THE WAY THAT
IT IS
CLIMATE
ACTION
NOW
LOVE

3

The Vanishing Polar Bear

Polar Bears are beautiful animals. They are unique in many ways, barely resembling their non-arctic counterparts. They have thick body fat necessary to survive in the Arctic. They feed on seals because there's not much else to feed on, and they spend about 50% of their time hunting for food.

In size, it most closely resembles the Kodiak Bear, and the male can reach over a thousand pounds in weight; females are about half that size. Their fur is a particular water-resistant type unique to their species.

Constantine John Phipps first recognized the polar bear as a unique species in 1744. The Inuit term for these magnificent creatures is Nanook.

Wikipedia: Compared with its closest relative, the brown bear, the polar bear has a more elongated body build and a longer skull and nose. As predicted by Allen's rule for a northerly animal, the legs are stocky, and the ears and tail are small. However, the feet are enormous to distribute load when walking on snow or thin ice and to provide propulsion when swimming; they may measure 30 cm (12 in) across in an adult. The pads of the paws are covered with small, soft papillae (dermal bumps), which provide traction on the ice. The polar bear's claws are short and stocky compared to the brown bear, perhaps to serve the former's need to grip heavy prey and ice. The claws are deeply scooped on the underside to assist in digging in the ice of the natural habitat. Research of injury patterns in polar bear forelimbs found injuries to the right forelimb more frequent than those to the left, suggesting right-handedness. Unlike the brown bear, polar bears in captivity are rarely overweight or particularly large, reacting to the warm conditions of most zoos.

The 42 teeth of a polar bear reflect its highly carnivorous diet. The cheek teeth are smaller and more jagged than the brown bear, and the canines are more prominent and sharper.

The Polar Bear is classified as a vulnerable species because of its habitat and concerns about climate change. For thousands of years, the polar bear has been a critical figure in circumpolar peoples' material, spiritual, and cultural life, and polar bears remain important in their cultures. Historically, the polar bear has also been known as the "white bear." (28)

But is the Polar Bear really in danger of extinction?

Polar bears are going extinct because of the loss of sea habitat from climate change. Polar bears have been threatened ever since May 2008. - Halle Wilson (29)

Because of the ongoing and potential loss of their sea ice habitat from climate change, polar bears were listed as a threatened species in the US under the Endangered Species Act in May 2008. – World Wildlife (30)

Polar bears will likely go extinct before the end of the 21st century. Polar Bear Facts (31)

There are currently 8 of the 19 species of Polar Bears out there with a status of vulnerable. This is due to the drop in their numbers and concerns that they will become extinct if that continues. Part of the problem has to do with the fact that Polar Bears were constantly hunted for decades. There were no restrictions, and the challenge of such a hunt inspired hunters worldwide. Polar Bear Endangered. (32)

In 2007, Grist published an article that claimed the polar bear population **could be extinct by 2030 if not 2020**! (emphasis mine) If realized, projected changes in future sea ice conditions will result in the loss of approximately 2/3 of the world's polar bear population by the mid-21st century. Because the observed trajectory of Arctic Sea ice decline appears to be underestimated by currently available models, this assessment of future polar bear status may be conservative.

This article discusses Michael Crichton's (a series global warming denier) review of Bjorn Lomborg's book *Cool It*. "Lomborg is only interested in real problems, and he has no patience with media fearmongering; he begins by dispatching the myth of the endangered polar bears, showing that this Disneyesque cartoon has no relevance to the real world where polar bear populations are increasing. Lomborg considers the issue in detail, citing sources from Al Gore to the World Wildlife Fund, then demonstrating that polar bear populations have increased fivefold since the 1960s." (33)

These sites list two reasons to be concerned about polar bears: being hunted and climate change. But where is the polar bear population? Is it in danger of going extinct by 2030 or 2020? Considering that it's now past 2020, we know it is invalid.

This does not stop the media machine from dispensing its propaganda to the masses. One video on the National Geographic site claims to have been viewed by 2.5 billion people and shows a polar bear starving and hunting for food on barren land. The implication is that it is dying because of climate change (34). Other claims are that pictures of polar bears on thin ice were photoshopped to promote that narrative.

But is the Polar Bear population shrinking or growing? The truth is that there are areas where the Polar Bear population is decreasing. Still, there are other areas where the population remains stable and the regions where the population is increasing. The climate crisis alarmists will use the figures from the decreasing areas to raise concern. In contrast, the climate crisis deniers will point to the places where the population is stable or even increasing to prove their point. The Polar Bear Population is around 25,000 – 30,000. (35)

The U.S. Fish and Wildlife Service estimates that the polar bear population is currently at 20,000 to 25,000 bears, up from as low as 5,000-10,000 bears in the 1950s and 1960s. A U.S. Geological Survey of Wildlife in the Arctic noted that the polar bear populations **'may now be near historic highs,'"** (emphasis mine) (36)

Climate Crisis alarmists are spreading their message.

IF THE CLIMATE
WAS A BANK
YOU WOULD HAVE
SAVED IT ALREADY

WE ARE DITCHING
SCHOOL
BECAUSE YOU
ARE DITCHING
OUR
FUTURE
It's
ecoLogy
it's not
ecoNomy

THE CLIMATE IS
CHANGING
SO SHOULD WE!
#ACTNOW

NO
NATURE
NO
FUTURE

STOP
COAL !
NOW

EARTH
IS MORE
valuablethanmoney

FIGHT TODAY
FOR A BETTER
TOMORROW

OUR PLANET
IS GETTING
HOTTER
THAN COLE
SPROUSE

Carbon, often misconstrued as the sole culprit, is a transparent gas. The real issue is global warming, a complex phenomenon that is less easily visible than carbon.

ONE
WORLD

There is
NO Planet B

4

The Father of Global Warming

James Hansen, the focus of this chapter, is often hailed as the Father of Global Warming. His work, which we will explore here, starkly contrasts with the global cooling scare that dominated the 1970s. Hansen's influential testimony to Congress redirected the narrative toward the emerging issue of *global warming*.

Wikipedia: The first NASA Goddard Institute for Space Studies (GISS) global temperature analysis was published in 1981. Hansen and his co-authors analyzed the surface air temperature at meteorological stations, focusing on 1880 to 1985. Temperatures for stations closer to one thousand kilometers were highly correlated, especially in the mid-latitudes, providing a way to combine the station data to provide accurate long-term variations.

They concluded that global mean temperatures can be determined even though meteorological stations are typically in the Northern Hemisphere and confined to continental regions. Warming in the past century was 0.5-0.7 °C, with warming similar in both hemispheres. When the analysis was updated in 1988, the four warmest years were in the 1980s. The two warmest years were 1981 and 1987.

During a senate meeting on June 23, 1988, Hansen reported that he was ninety-nine percent certain the earth was warmer then than it had ever been measured to be, that there was a clear cause-and-effect relationship with the greenhouse effect, and that due to global warming, the likelihood of freak weather was steadily increasing.

With the 1991 eruption of Mount Pinatubo, 1992 saw a cooling in global temperatures. There was speculation that this would cause the next couple of years to be more relaxed because of the sizeable serial correlation in the global temperatures. Bassett and Lin found the statistical odds of a new temperature record to be small. Hansen countered by saying that having insider information shifted the odds to those who know the physics of the climate system and that whether there is a new temperature record depends upon the data set used.

Hansen's career is marked by a series of intriguing predictions that have piqued the interest of the scientific community and the public's interest.

Increased tornado activity.

More severe hurricanes.

A cause-and-effect relationship between the greenhouse effect and observed warming.

Most of Greenland's ice would melt, causing sea levels to rise 23 feet over the next hundred years.

The west side highway (which runs along the Hudson River) will be underwater.

Mr. Hansen then drew up three scenarios that were futures since 1988. Which is the closest in reality? Let's look:

"Business as usual," as it maintained the accelerating emissions growth typical of the 1970s and '80s. This scenario predicted the earth would warm 1 degree Celsius by 2018.

This scenario set emissions lower, rising at the same rate today as in 1988. Mr. Hansen called this outcome the **most plausible** and predicted it would lead to about 0.7 degrees of warming by this year. (emphasis mine both times)

He deemed this scenario **highly unlikely**: constant emissions beginning in 2000. In that forecast, temperatures would rise a few tenths of a degree before flatlining after 2000.

Which of these scenarios happened? It was the one that Hansen said was highly unlikely; that's correct. c) It was the one that occurred.

Thirty years of data have been collected since Mr. Hansen outlined his scenarios—enough to determine which was closest to reality. And the winner is Scenario C. Global surface temperature has not increased significantly since 2000, discounting the larger-than-usual El Niño of 2015-16. Assessed by Mr. Hansen's model, surface temperatures behave as if we had capped 18 years ago the carbon dioxide emissions responsible for the enhanced greenhouse effect. But we did not. And it is not just Mr. Hansen who got it wrong. Models devised by the United Nations Intergovernmental Panel on Climate Change have, on average, predicted about twice as much warming as observed since global satellite temperature monitoring began 40 years ago. - Climatologist Dr. Pat Michaels and Meteorologist Dr. Ryan Maue - June 21, 2018. (52)

Another disturbing thing about Mr. Hansen is how he testified before Congress in 1988. In an interview with former Colorado Senator Timothy Wirth: *"Believe it or not, we called the Weather Bureau and found out what historically was the hottest day of the summer. It was stiflingly hot that summer. [At] the same time, you had this drought across the country, so the linkage between the Hansen hearing and the drought became very intense.*

... What we did was go in the night before and open all the windows, I will admit, right? So, the air conditioning wasn't working inside the room, and when the hearing occurred, there was not only bliss, which is television cameras in double figures, but it was sweltering. ...

So, Hansen's giving this testimony, you've got these television cameras back there heating the room, and the air conditioning in the room didn't appear to work. So, it was a perfect collection of events that happened that day, with the wonderful Jim Hansen wiping his brow at the witness table and giving this remarkable testimony. ..." (53)

The air conditioning was rigged that day, so it wouldn't work, or at least not fixed, giving credence to Mr. Hansen's testimony.

LESS MEAT
LESS HEAT
#Ecolocaust
@ExxonShell
CLIMATE JUSTICE

5

An Inconvenient Propaganda Piece

We examined the Leonard Nimoy narrated In Search of The Coming Ice Age in a previous chapter. I want to explore and review former Vice President Al Gore's *An Inconvenient Truth* in this chapter. However, the Leonard Nimoy show was only half an hour long, and Al Gore's was over an hour and a half, so my examination of his movie wouldn't be as in-depth. (37)

The film opens with Al Gore narrating a video of a river. At one point, Mr. Gore claims that this film is nonpartisan but opens with the statement, "I am Al Gore. I used to be the next President of the United States of America." Then, we're treated to a montage of him on the campaign trail. That's followed by a montage of devastation caused by nature.

Gore then jokes about his geology teacher becoming a science advisor in the current (Bush) administration. He then quotes Mark Twain (ironically): "What gets us into trouble is not what we don't know. It's what we know for sure that ain't so."

Gore then provides an introductory science lesson on how the sun heats the Earth, enhancing the audience's understanding. He supplements this with a video presentation, Global Warming or None Like It Hot, which suggests that politicians can contribute to the solution. He introduces Dr. Roger Revelle, one of his college professors who sparked his interest in global warming. Revelle was the first to propose measuring carbon dioxide in the Earth's atmosphere. They experimented in 1957, tracking the amount of CO2 entering the atmosphere using weather balloons.

Of course, we know that as the industrial age advanced, the amount of CO2 man put into the atmosphere did, indeed, increase. However, as we saw earlier, the total amount of CO2 man has put into Earth's atmosphere is only 0.04 percent of the total CO2 put into the air. Even if man doubled the amount he was putting into the atmosphere, it would still be less than one percent of the total CO2 that goes into Earth's atmosphere.

Then, the former vice president details the history of his political career while striving to raise awareness of global warming. He demonstrates how glaciers are shrinking and predicts that no more snow will be on Kilimanjaro within a decade. This emphasis on the issue's urgency engages the audience and encourages them to be part of the solution.

That was 2006, so in 2016, there should have been no snow on Mount Kilimanjaro. It is now 2024, and if you look at a satellite picture of Mount Kilimanjaro, there is still snow. Error number one in the film.

What could be an explanation for why the snow retreated on the mount back in 2006? Was it, in fact, global warming?

Anthony Watts provides this explanation: *I've said many times that Kilimanjaro's loss of ice cover involves sublimation, not warming. The picture of Thompson next to the sliver of ice proves it. Note there's no meltwater near him. That sliver is a symptom of sublimation – ice evaporating directly into the air like ice cubes shrink when left in the freezer too long.* (38)

Mr. Gore continues to show the retreating glaciers from the 1980s to 2006. It's interesting to contrast what Mr. Nimoy said in 1978 with what Mr. Gore said in 2006. Through newspaper clippings, we saw what the "experts" said in 1978: that we were approaching another ice age. Then, Mr. Gore's lecture tells us that the ice is retreating, and we're in danger of the glaciers melting.

Then, the former Vice President showed us a correlation between temperature and CO2 over the past 1,000 years. The implication is that correlation equals causation: as CO2 emissions increased, so did the temperature. However, they conveniently skip the freezing cold temperatures that we already looked at during the 1970s, when mankind's CO2 emissions dramatically increased since the Dust Bowl era of the 1930s.

Then Mr. Gore presents a chart that represents co-relation, which leads to causation between rising temperatures in the past 650,000 years. However, Mr. Gore leaves out a lot of information in his little presentation: *...Presents a graph tracking CO2 levels and global temperatures during the past 650,000 years, but never mentions the most significant point: Global temperatures were warmer than the present during each of the past four interglacial periods, even though CO2 levels were lower.* (39)

After his lecture about CO2 and temperature, he says that the temperature will continue to rise over the next 50 years as CO2 levels increase. The temperatures have been cooling, not to a great degree, but they still haven't risen sharply as predicted in the film. *There's no correlation between CO2 and temperature.*

"Twentieth-century global warming did not start until 1910. By then, CO2 emissions had already risen from the expanded use of coal that had powered the Industrial Revolution, and emissions only increased slowly from 3.5 gigatons in 1910 to under four gigatons by the end of the Second World War.

It was post-war industrialization that caused the rapid rise in global CO2 emissions. Still, by 1945, when this began, the Earth was already in a cooling phase, which started around 1942 and continued until 1975. With 32 years of rapidly increasing global temperatures and only a minor increase in global CO2 emissions, followed by 33 years of slowly cooling global temperatures with rapid increases in global CO2 emissions, it was deceitful for the IPCC to make any claim that CO2 emissions were primarily responsible for observed 20th-century global warming." (Norm Kalmanovitch). (40)

After claiming that this wasn't a political issue but a moral one, he discusses a tragic disaster that happened to his son. Then, the discussion turns to the ten hottest years on earth. The rise of temperatures in our oceans causes more severe storms. We also look at Hurricanes that happened in the early 2000s.

After this, we look at the Presidential election 2000 (I thought this wasn't about politics, lol). Then, it's back to a montage of more storm disasters and personal recollections. Then, Mr. Gore talks about how the North Pole has lost 40 percent of its ice in 40 years.

Again, in 1978, the fear was another ice age covering the world in ice; in 2006, it became a fear of the ice melting and causing the seas and oceans to rise. The lecture tells us that ice from the Arctic reflects the sun's rays into space, but the oceans of the Arctic absorb the sun's rays, causing it to get hotter. Then, the discussion reverts to polar bears, which we discussed in a previous chapter.

The discussion then turns to the ocean's currents. And what happened to Europe during its last ice age? Mr. Gore says we are the worst contributors to the problem (he says while a video of him at an airport is playing, boarding an airplane, which contributes to the C02 emissions into the atmosphere, Mr. Gore? Hmmm. At least Greta Thunberg refuses to fly, showing she believes in her message).

Then, there's yet another political montage, starting with a quote from Ronald Reagan about the haze on the Smoky Mountains—this in a film that's supposed to be nonpartisan.

The conversation changes how global warming affects people physically, with new species rising, diseases running rampant, and other species going extinct at an alarming rate.

Then, Mr. Gore discusses the ice breakup in Antarctica, the planet's most enormous mass of ice by far. He looks at how the ice shelves are breaking up, focusing on Larson B.   According to the lecture, sea levels will rise twenty feet if we lose this ice shelf. Then, he compares it to Greenland. If we lose Greenland, sea levels will also rise twenty feet. Then, he shows us the devastation if Antarctica and Greenland were to melt.

Then we go to China, where Mr. Gore discusses the amount of coal burning that China is doing and how this is contributing to air pollution. After that, the population explosion since the baby boom generation is discussed, from 2.5 billion people to over 6 billion.

The discussion then changes to what we can do to prevent catastrophes that will theoretically occur due to global warming. He also shows us how the various continents of this world disperse CO2 into the atmosphere, and of course, the USA is the biggest culprit, putting 30.3 percent into the atmosphere.

Then he compares the global warming crisis to the smoking crisis, the surgeon general's report that shows a correlation between smoking and lung cancer. Then, another personal story of how he lost his sister, Nancy, to cancer. Al Gore Sr. was a tobacco farmer, and after his daughter died, he stopped growing tobacco. The correlation is that he had to connect the dots and realize that his profession contributed to the death of Nancy. They wish they had connected the dots sooner.

Now we come to the famous moment that states that 97 percent of all scientists claim that humankind contributes to global warming. He goes on to argue that scientists who refute this are working for the oil and coal industry as well as the white house, again bringing partisan politics into a supposedly nonpartisan program.

After all of that, he shows how he's been jetting around the world, giving the same lecture to different groups before compiling it all into a movie.

The wrap-up includes comparing our automobile standards to those of other countries and pointing out that we have the knowledge to combat the problems he presents in this lecture. He shows us how, even though we as a nation are not stepping up to the plate, individual cities are pledging to support Kyoto.

First, let's discuss the melting ice in Greenland. Is there cause for alarm? We can find alarmists from many years ago talking about the melting glaciers.

Is the Arctic climate becoming more temperate? The famous Swedish gave remarkable new information authority, Professor H. W. Ahlmann in a lecture to the Swedish Geographical Society, suggests that this may be the case.

Professor Ahlmann was speaking on the collated results of his expedition to northeast Greenland. He stated that the glaciers there showed clear signs of a change towards a warmer climate. As had been observed in other parts of the Arctic, especially in Spitzbergen, the melting had increased rapidly.

By far, the most significant number of local glaciers in northeast Greenland had receded considerably during recent decades, and it would not be an exaggeration to say that these glaciers were nearing a catastrophe. (41)

So, there we were in 1940, with glaciers melting at an unprecedented rate and government scientists scaring us back then before the term *global warming* even existed. But is today's glacier melting any worse than what happened back then?

Dr Olsen's colleague Ruth Mottram, an expert on Greenland's ice sheet, told The Independent the onset of hot temperatures combined with very few cracks in the ice meant the rapid accumulation of meltwater could not drain through the solid ice sheet.

"Last week saw the onset of hot conditions in Greenland and much of the rest of the Arctic, driven by warmer air moving up from the south."

She added: "The DMI weather station nearby at Qaanaaq airport registered a high of 17.3C on Wednesday and 15C on Thursday, which is pretty warm for Northern Greenland, even in summer!"

Greenland is currently experiencing near-record levels of ice melt, with the country losing more than two gigatons (equal to 2 billion tons) of ice on that day alone.

The sudden spike in melting "is unusual, but not unprecedented" *(emphasis mine), Thomas Mote, a research scientist at the University of Georgia who studies Greenland's climate, told CNN.*

"It is comparable to some spikes we saw in <u>June 2012,</u>" he said.

That year saw record-setting ice melt, with almost the entire ice sheet experiencing melting for the first time in recorded history. (42)

If you study the history of Greenland's melting in the summer, you will see that it was more severe in 2012 than this past year. You see, snow melts every summer. (43) The temperature in Greenland today is 53 degrees, and tonight's low will be 37 degrees. Which is normal for this time of year. (01/16/2020)

Now, I want to discuss 97% of all scientists. I will direct you to the presentation by **<u>Dr. John Robson</u>** (44). He begins with then-President Obama's quote in 2013: "97% of all scientists agree climate change is real, manmade and dangerous." John Kerry expanded that by stating that "97% of the world's scientists…" followed by a CNN quote…you get the picture.

Dr. Robson acknowledges that you don't need a poll to tell you that C02 is a greenhouse gas and will likely have some warming effects. After that, he discusses that the world is warmer after the end of a natural cooling period called *the Little Ice Age*. He also acknowledges that man has changed his environment by putting things he shouldn't into the sea and air. Most would agree with that.

The points of contention are whether humans are the only cause of global warming or whether climate change is a dangerous threat.

The idea of a 97 percent consensus seems to have begun with Naomi Oreskes (45), who, in 2004, claimed to have surveyed 928 papers on the subject, and 75 percent came to the consensus that earth's climate was being affected by human activities and none directly disputed it. By 2006, Mr. Gore had morphed that number to the typical 97 percent number, but no one knows how he came to that conclusion since the only study said 75 percent of scientists said that man might have something to do with affecting the climate.

So, where does the 97 – 98 percent consensus come from? A survey done by two University of Illinois researchers sent out 10,000 e-mails to earth scientists and asked two simple questions:

Do you agree that global temperatures have generally risen since the pre-1800's?

Do you think that human activity is a significant contributing factor?

That's it. There is no mention of any crisis, global warming, greenhouse gases, or anything of that nature. Is human activity a contributing factor? This is the survey that *proves* man's involvement with global warming. Very few that quote that number even know where the survey comes from or what the questions on the survey were, despite there being only two questions asked.

Less than half of those who were surveyed responded. 10,257 questionnaires were sent, and 3,146 responded. Of those who responded, 90 percent said yes to the first question, and 82 percent said yes to the second question. However, among meteorologists, you know, those that study the weather, only 64 percent said yes to the second question, no crisis, no danger, and barely more than half of those that research weather conditions felt that man had contributed anything to the warming of the last century or so. (46)

So, where does that 97 percent number come from? Well, of the 77 who described themselves as climate experts, 75 said yes to that second question, which means that 97 percent of less than 80 scientists believe that man is somehow, but with no specifics, involved in the warming of the earth. That's 77 out of 3,146 that responded. That's hardly 97 percent of the world's scientists, just 97 percent of less than 2 percent that answered the survey.

Now we come to the Cook report, another report claiming that 97 percent of scientists believed that man was responsible for global warming...or does it?

Wikipedia: **John Cook** theoretically examined 11,944 abstracts from peer-reviewed scientific literature from 1991–2011 that matched the topics 'global climate change' or 'global warming.' They found that, while 66.4% of them expressed no position on anthropogenic global warming (AGW), of those that did, 97.1% endorsed the consensus position that humans are contributing to global warming. They also invited authors to rate their papers and found that, while 35.5% rated their paper as expressing no position on AGW, 97.2% of the rest endorsed the consensus.

In both cases, the percentage of endorsements among papers expressing a position marginally increased over time. They concluded that the number of papers rejecting the consensus on AGW is a small proportion of the published research. (47) That's **two-thirds** (emphasis mine) of the papers expressing no opinion, and of the ones that did express an opinion, **less than a third**. (emphasis mine) expressed an opinion, and of that 34 percent expressed an opinion, 33 percent believed man to have contributed to global warming, but they did not all agree as to what extent man played a role in global warming 33 from 34 equals 97 percent.

That begs the question: How many papers surveyed claim that humans have caused most of the observed global warming? Only 64 of 12,000 papers claimed humans caused global warming. Dr. Robson is right; that's not 97 percent; that's one-half of one percent.

Now, let's look at the American Meteorological Society's internal poll of its members. They surveyed 7,000 members and received 1,800 responses.

Fifty-two percent said that global warming is happening and is primarily man-made. The rest either didn't know, said it wasn't happening, or that it was happening, but man had nothing to do with its results. (48)

In this video, Dr. Robson discusses another report by the <u>Netherlands Environmental Agency</u>. It shows that 66 percent of those surveyed believe man is involved with global warming. However, in addition to scientists, they also surveyed psychologists, pollsters, philosophers, and poll takers. This tells us that many people in this survey are not experts, which somewhat nullifies their results.

Toward the end of this video, Dr. Robson quotes scientist Jose Duarte. It is worth repeating here:

"It is ill-advised to report a consensus as an aggregation of independent judgments. Humans are an ultrasocial species, and dissent is far costlier than assent to a perceived majority.

A scientist who contests the prevailing narrative on human-caused warming or merely produces smaller estimates will likely end up on a McCarthyite blacklist of "deniers."

Self-described mainstream climate scientists refer the public to such lists, implicitly endorsing the smearing of their colleagues. This is disturbing and unheard of in other sciences.

Have hurricanes increased or decreased in intensity?

QUEERS & FEMINISTS DEMAND CLIMATE JUSTICE

SAVE THE PLANET
NO PLASTIC

SAVE THE PLANET

CLIMATE
CRISIS
WAKE
UP
DISOBEY

LESS
MEAT
LESS
HEAT

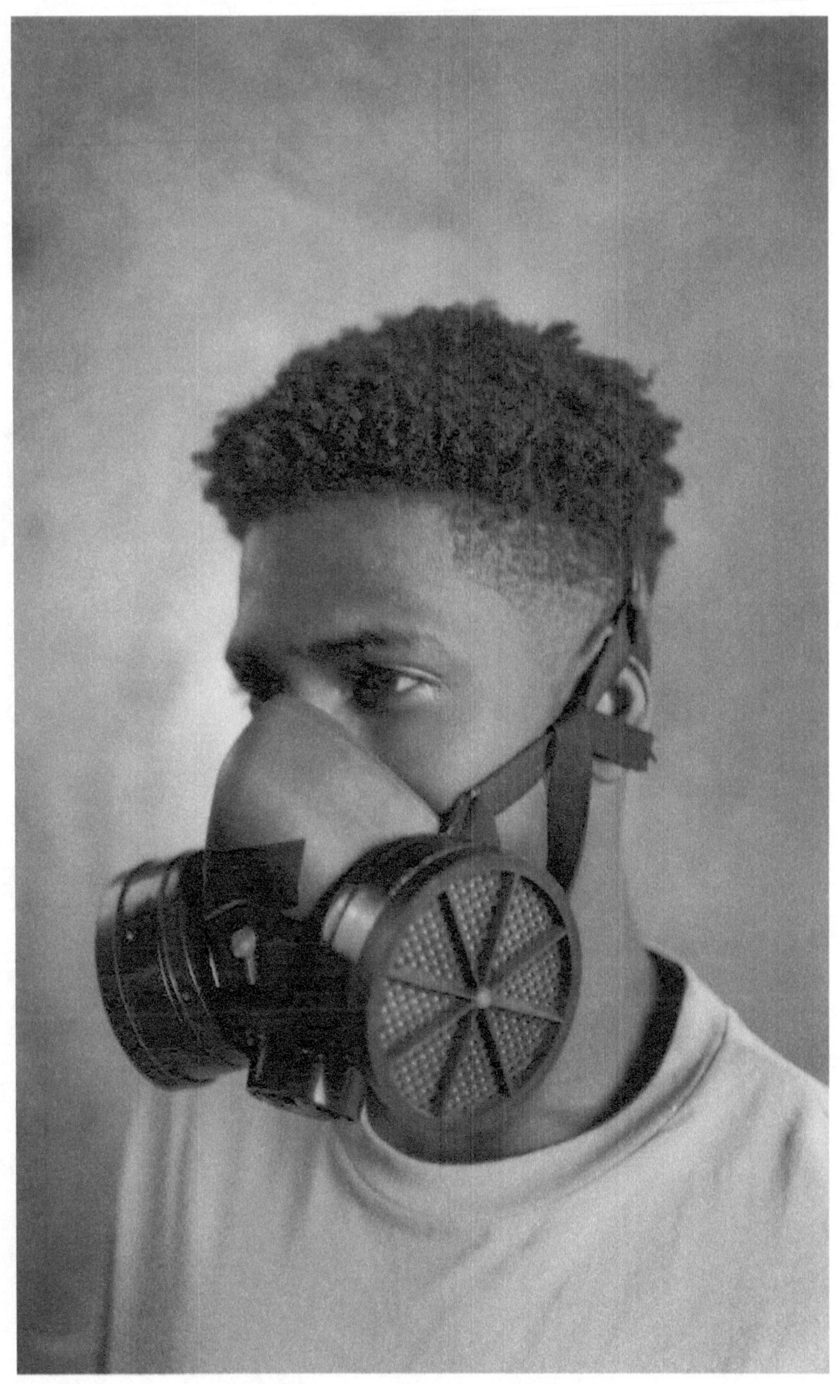

6

Vacationing Under Water
(Don't Interrupt the Cabinet Meeting)

Have you ever wanted to vacation on the Maldives Islands? An exotic tropical resort is known mainly for its tourism. The only problem is that they're underwater. At least, according to the climate alarmists, they're supposed to be.

A gradual rise in average sea level is threatening to completely cover this Indian Ocean nation of 1196 small islands within the next 30 (2018) years, according to authorities. The Environmental

Affairs Director, Mr. Hussein Shihab, said an estimated rise of 20 to 30 centimeters in the next 20 to 40 years could be "catastrophic" for most of the islands, which were no more than a meter above sea level. The United Nations Environment Project was planning a study of the problem. But the end of the Maldives and its 200,000 people could come sooner if drinking water supplies dry up by 1992, as predicted. (50)

The Canberra Times has a history of gloomy climate predictions. I'm not going to share the articles, which pretty much all say the same thing, but let's look at some headlines and excerpts.

<u>**World Temperature Has Fallen**</u>

"...climatologists say they expect to see ice floes continuing to close in around Iceland - January 24, 1970

<u>**A New Ice Age Could Grip the World...**</u>

...International scientists have changed their minds (they change their minds as often as the climate changes) about the speed with which the world's 'weather machine' can change gear. - November 22, 1974.

<u>**The Ice Age Cometh**</u>

Some scientists believe a new ice age is on the way. Others insist it has already begun - May 31st, 1975

Throughout the '70, the " experts " predicted that the Maldives would be underwater.

The scare was so great that the President of this island country held an underwater cabinet meeting. Wait, what? That's right. This is a publicity stunt to raise awareness of climate change.

Under the threat of that looming watery Armageddon, President Mohamed Nasheed has announced plans to hold a cabinet meeting under the sea ahead of the UN climate change conference in Copenhagen this December.

Ministers clad in wetsuits and shouldering compressed-air tanks will meet about 20 feet (6m) underwater on 17 October. According to Aminath Shauna, an official from the president's office, they will communicate through hand gestures.

Advertisement:

"It is to send a message to the world. The intention is to draw the attention of the world leaders to the issue of global warming and highlight how serious the threats faced by Maldives as a result," she said. "If we can stop climate change, the lowest-lying nation on earth will be saved." The gathering will take place off

the island of Girifushi, which lies about a 20-minute journey by speedboat from the capital, Male. (51)

Ok, that was quite the publicity stunt. We can only guess his motive was to raise cash for a perceived crisis.

The Maldives are a tropical paradise!

All 1,196 islands are still above water after more than 40 years of doom and gloom prophesies.

THERE ARE
NO JOBS
ON A
DEAD PLANET.
ver.di JUGEND

7

Alexandria Ocasio-Cortez, Greta Thunberg and modern politics

"Climate change is here + we've got a deadline: 12 years left to cut emissions in half." – Alexandria Ocasio-Cortez.

AOC has made many wild claims concerning the so-called climate crisis, from cattle flatulence to the idea that we should stop having babies. It all concerned the Green New Deal, which she desperately tried to push through Congress not too long ago. Fortunately, it didn't go anywhere. The climate alarmists were constantly trying to get us to give up money to combat the so-called crises. They also want us to give up basic food and energy sources for their absurd claims.

We've already seen that temperature rising and falling throughout the 20th century had nothing to do with how much carbon mankind put into the atmosphere. We've discussed the Dust Bowl situation of the 1930s, but I didn't mention in that chapter how the ice at the poles and in Greenland melted away during that decade and into the 1950s.

*In his seminal 1982 book Climate, History, and the Modern World, the renowned climatologist **Dr. H.H. Lamb** revealed that sea ice in the subarctic and Arctic regions was much less extensive* *during the Medieval Warm Period (9th-13th centuries) than today.*

For example, records indicate decadal and centennial-scale periods without sea ice invading Iceland's coasts. These no-ice periods coincided with atmospheric CO2 concentrations of 275 ppm, about 130 ppm less than today's calculated CO2 values.

Climate models are predicated on the presumption that the higher the CO2 concentration, the greater the sea ice loss. These long-term trends strongly suggest that CO2 concentration changes are not the modulators of polar sea ice changes they claim to be. (55)

In 1963, we saw the trend start to reverse, not just at the poles and Greenland but elsewhere, too.

*According to glaciologist Mr. **Olav Liestol**, Norway's glaciers are gradually melting again after 200 years of gradually increasing thickness.*

Last year, nearly all glaciers increased by more than one meter – approximately four feet. (56)

Looking at all the evidence presented in this volume, we do not have to worry about how much C02 man puts into the atmosphere. It is incredible how many people buy into these doomsday scenarios without looking into the evidence presented online. Of course, part of the problem is that you must sift through many lies and half-truths to get to the truth. Politicians, as we have seen, are incredibly guilty of disinformation.

Does Alexandria Ocasio-Cortez present any actual evidence to support her claims? Yet she is determined to push through her Green New Deal, which would cost so much money, is unnecessary, and may hurt the environment, as C02 is good for plant life, and food production may have increased due to an increase in C02 in the atmosphere. (57)

It is no secret that the current Democratic presidential candidates are all talking about climate change, thanks partly to Cortez's efforts. Their views vary wildly on the importance of climate control, but they all want to placate the left wing of their party.

Republican Senator Rand Paul has taken to taunting AOC on Twitter: "No @AOC, the world will not end in 12 years, but we must, absolutely must do something, over the next 500 million years,"

AOC has fired back since claiming that Rand took her quote out of context and compared the GOP climate plan to the Mel Brooks movie *Spaceballs*. In the film, the planet Druidia is surrounded by a force field that protects its atmosphere. All this climate chatter is undoubtedly entertaining but does not get any closer to a proper understanding of the relationship, if any, that CO_2 plays in the world's climate.

Now we come to Time's Person of the Year for 2019...

Greta Thunberg is a sophomore in high school, or at least should be in high school. Instead, she's being paraded around the globe as if she's the second coming of Christ for the climate alarmists.

I am so baffled by this. What is a 17-year-old girl going to do about the climate? Does she have information that we don't have? Is she some savant who will present a secret formula to handle all the world's climate problems? I think the answer lies within the political strategy. After all, how many of you heartless denizens would criticize a child?

The Greta Thunberg cult is growing!

Wikipedia: Greta Tintin Eleonora Ernman Thunberg (born 3 January 2003) is a Swedish environmental activist on climate change whose campaigning has gained international recognition. Thunberg is known for her straightforward manner of speaking, both in public and to political leaders and assemblies, in which she urges immediate action to address what she describes as the climate crisis.

Thunberg first became known for youth activism in August 2018 when, at age 15, she began spending her school days outside the Swedish parliament to call for more decisive action on climate change by holding up a sign reading Skolstrejk för klimatet (School strike for the climate).

Soon, other students engaged in similar protests in their communities. They organized a school climate strike movement called Fridays for the Future. After Thunberg addressed the 2018 United Nations Climate Change Conference, student strikes occurred every week worldwide. In 2019, at least two coordinated multi-city protests involving over 1,000,000 students each. At home, Thunberg convinced her parents to adopt several lifestyle choices to reduce their carbon footprint, including giving up air travel and not eating meat.

Her sudden rise to world fame has made her a leader and a target. In May 2019, Thunberg was featured on the cover of Time magazine, which named her a "next generation leader" and said that many see her as a role model. Thunberg and the school strike movement were also featured in a 30-minute Vice documentary titled Make the World Greta Again. Some media have described her impact on the world stage as the "Greta effect."

Thunberg has received many honors and awards, including an honorary fellowship from the Royal Scottish Geographical Society. In 2019, Time magazine named her one of the 100 most influential people and the youngest individual Time Person of the Year. In September 2019, she addressed the UN Climate Action

Summit in New York. Thunberg was also nominated for the 2019 Nobel Peace Prize. (58)

Some people have accused me of making fun of Greta; on the contrary! I do not mock her but criticize the media's obsession with her. I feel deeply sorry for Ms. Thunberg. I wholeheartedly agree with what she said during her speech: "<u>This is all wrong. I shouldn't be up here. I should be back in school on the other side of the ocean.</u> Yet you all come to us young people for hope? How dare you! You have stolen my dreams and my childhood with your empty words. And yet, I'm one of the lucky ones. People are suffering. People are dying. Entire ecosystems are collapsing. We are in the beginning of a mass extinction. And all you can talk about is money and fairytales of eternal economic growth. How dare you!" (59)

She should be back in school. Her childhood has been robbed. Not by the people she thinks it's been stolen by, however. Her childhood was robbed by the people who exploited her for political gain, beginning with her parents.

Speaking of cutting schools, it is wrong to allow our high school students to cut schools for some bogus climate crisis. How many high school students who are cutting class care about the political reasoning for this? So many students are probably just using this excuse to get out of school for a day and have a three-day weekend.

Greta isn't the only high school student who political activists have exploited. David Hogg, before her, was used by the Gun Control Lobby to speak out against owning weapons after the Stoneman Douglas High School Shooting.

Greta has been so criticized on Facebook that she has threatened to leave the social media giant if they don't stop attacking her. I find it sad when people criticize her, but her claims should be criticized and scrutinized, especially when no evidence is presented to back them up.

Thunberg and her followers are prepared to tell Davis's investors and policymakers to stop investing in fossil fuels. They will demand action now.

They understand that the world is complicated but claim that the climate crisis is tricky. They go on to claim the fact this hasn't happened is a disgrace. Then, they point out that since the 2015 Paris Agreement, 33 central global banks have collectively poured $1.9tn into fossil fuels. They also claim that "Anything less than immediately ceasing these investments in the fossil fuel industry would be a betrayal of life itself." (61)

The followers' fight is so real and impassioned, and they are almost religious in their determination. They are bringing lawsuits against those they believe are responsible for the climate crises. Thankfully, common sense prevails, and these suits are being thrown out of court.

From the New York Times: *A federal judge has rejected New York City's lawsuit to help fossil fuel companies pay the costs of dealing with climate change.*

Judge John F. Keenan of the United States District Court for the Southern District of New York wrote that climate change must be addressed by the executive branch and Congress, not by the courts.

While climate change "is a fact of life," Judge Keenan wrote, "the serious problems caused thereby are not for the judiciary to ameliorate. The two other branches of government must address global warming and solutions to that."

The 23-page decision is a second defeat for local and state governments seeking to use the judiciary to address problems caused by climate change. The first was in a case brought by San Francisco and Oakland that Judge William H. Alsup of the Federal District Court in San Francisco threw out last month. (62)

I have no animosity towards Greta and am sorry for Ms. Thunberg. Her passion is real, and I respect certain decisions she has made, including not flying, because of her desire to help the world she lives in.

But I believe she is misguided and must learn that there are many views as to how much mankind's involvement in climate is affecting our globe. I recognize that she is being manipulated and exploited by the adult world, beginning with her parents, to hopefully, desperately strike an emotional chord in the hearts of anyone who will listen to her.

She has no actual knowledge of the effects of greenhouse gases. Indeed, most of us do not. Yes, CO_2 is a greenhouse gas, and some heat is reradiated back to the earth's surface because of it, but to what extent, we don't know. That's why the predictions about climate have been mostly wrong, as we've pointed out, and climate models always fail. They fail because they do not consider all the variables.

Mark Simone of WOR Radio has concocted his list of 120 climate scares from the alarmists. I want to share it with you now:

Scientists seeking funding and journalists seeking an audience agree: panic sells. "Global cooling is going to kill us all! No, wait, global warming is going to kill us all!" Here's the list - a fantastic chronology of the last 120 years of scaremongering on climate:

1895 - Geologists Think the World May Be Frozen Up Again – New York Times, February 1895.

1902 - "Disappearing Glaciers...deteriorating slowly, with a persistency that means their final annihilation...scientific fact...surely disappearing." – Los Angeles Times.

1912 - Prof. Schmidt Warns Us of an Encroaching Ice Age – New York Times, October 1912.

1923 - "Scientist says Arctic ice will wipe out Canada" – Professor Gregory of Yale University, American representative to the Pan-Pacific Science Congress, – Chicago Tribune.

1923 - "The discoveries of changes in the sun's heat and the southward advance of glaciers in recent years have given rise to conjectures of the possible advent of a new ice age" – Washington Post.

1924 - MacMillan Reports Signs of New Ice Age – New York Times, Sept 18, 1924.

1929 - "Most geologists think the world is growing warmer, and that it will continue to get warmer" – Los Angeles Times, in Is another ice age coming?

1932 - "If these things be true, it is evident, therefore that we must be just teetering on an ice age" – The Atlantic magazine, This Cold, Cold World.

1933 - America in Longest Warm Spell Since 1776; Temperature Line Records a 25-Year Rise – New York Times, March 27th, 1933.

1933 – "...wide-spread and persistent tendency toward warmer weather...Is our climate changing?" – Federal Weather Bureau "Monthly Weather Review."

1938 - Global warming, caused by man heating the planet with carbon dioxide, "is likely to prove beneficial to mankind in several ways, besides the provision of heat and power."– Quarterly Journal of the Royal Meteorological Society.

1938 - "Experts puzzle over 20-year mercury rise...Chicago is in the front rank of thousands of cities throughout the world which have been affected by a mysterious trend toward warmer climate in the last two decades" – Chicago Tribune.

1939 - "Gaffers who claim that winters were harder when they were boys are quite right... weathermen have no doubt that the world at least for the time being is growing warmer" – Washington Post.

1952 - "...we have learned that the world has been getting warmer in the last half century" – New York Times, August 10th, 1962.

1954 - "...winters are getting milder, summers drier. Glaciers are receding, deserts growing" – U.S. News and World Report.

1954 - Climate – the Heat May Be Off – Fortune Magazine.

1959 - "Arctic Findings in Particular Support Theory of Rising Global Temperatures" – New York Times.

1969 - "...the Arctic pack ice is thinning and that the ocean at the North Pole may become an open sea within a decade or two" – New York Times, February 20th, 1969.

1969 – "If I were a gambler, I would take even money that England will not exist in the year 2000" — Paul Ehrlich (while he now predicts doom from global warming, this quote only gets an honorable mention, as he was talking about his crazy fear of overpopulation).

1970 - "...get a good grip on your long johns, cold weather haters – the worst may be yet to come...there's no relief in sight" – Washington Post.

1974 - Global cooling for the past forty years – Time Magazine.

1974 - "Climatological Cassandras are becoming increasingly apprehensive, for the weather aberrations they are studying may be the harbinger of another ice age" –Washington Post.

1974 - "As for the present cooling trend several leading climatologists have concluded that it is very bad news indeed" – Fortune magazine, which won a Science Writing Award from the American Institute of Physics for its analysis of the danger.

1974 - "...the facts of the present climate change are such that the most optimistic experts would assign near certainty to major crop failure...mass deaths by starvation, and probably anarchy and violence" – New York Times.

1975 - **Scientists Ponder Why World's Climate is Changing; A Major Cooling Widely Considered to Be Inevitable** – New York Times, May 21st, 1975.

1975 - **"The threat of a new ice age must now stand alongside nuclear war as a likely source of wholesale death and misery for mankind"** - Nigel Calder, editor of New Scientist magazine, in an article in International Wildlife Magazine.

1976 - **"Even U.S. farms may be hit by cooling trend"** – U.S. News and World Report.

1981 - **Global Warming** – **"of an almost unprecedented magnitude"** – New York Times.

1988 - I would like to draw three main conclusions. **Number one**, the earth was warmer in 1988 than ever in the history of instrumental measurements. **Number two**, global warming is now large enough to ascribe a cause-and-effect relationship to the greenhouse effect with a high degree of confidence. And **number three**, our computer climate simulations indicate that the greenhouse effect is already significant enough to affect the probability of extreme events such as summer heat waves. – Jim Hansen, in June 1988, during a testimony before Congress, see His later quote and His superior's objection for context.

1989 - "On the one hand, as scientists, we are ethically bound to the scientific method, in effect promising to tell the truth, the whole truth, and nothing but – which means that we must include all doubts, the caveats, the ifs, ands or buts. On the other hand, we are not just scientists but human beings as well. And like most people, we'd like to see the world as a better place, which in this context translates into our working to reduce the risk of potentially disastrous climate change. To do that, we need broad support to capture the public's imagination. That, of course, means getting loads of media coverage. So, we have to offer up scary scenarios, make simplified, dramatic statements, and make little mention of any doubts we might have.

This "double ethical bind" we frequently find ourselves in cannot be solved by any formula. Each of us must decide the right balance between being effective and honest. I hope that means being both." – Stephen Schneider, lead author of the Intergovernmental Panel on Climate Change, Discover magazine, October 1989.

1990 - "We've got to ride the global warming issue. Even if the theory of global warming is wrong, we will be doing the right thing – regarding economic and environmental policy" – Senator Timothy Wirth.

1993 - "Global climate change may alter temperature and rainfall patterns, many scientists fear, with uncertain consequences for agriculture." – U.S. News and World Report.

1998 - No matter if the science [of global warming] is all phony . . . climate change [provides] the greatest opportunity to bring about justice and equality in the world." —Christine Stewart, Canadian Minister of the Environment, Calgary Herald, 1998.

2001 - "Scientists no longer doubt that global warming is happening, and almost nobody questions the fact that humans are at least partly responsible." – Time Magazine, Monday, Apr. 09, 2001.

2003 - Emphasis on extreme scenarios may have been appropriate at one time, when the public and decision-makers were relatively unaware of the global warming issue, and energy sources such as "synfuels," shale oil, and tar sands were receiving strong consideration" – Jim Hansen, NASA Global Warming activist, can we defuse The Global Warming Time Bomb? 2003.

2006 - "I believe it is appropriate to have an over-representation of factual presentations on how dangerous it is, as a predicate for opening up the audience to listen to what the solutions are, and how hopeful it is that we are going to solve this crisis." — Al Gore, Grist magazine, May 2006.

2006 – "It is not a debate over whether the earth has been warming over the past century. The earth is always warming or cooling, at least a few tenths of a degree…" —Richard S. Lindzen, the Alfred P. Sloan professor of meteorology at MIT.

2006 – "What we have fundamentally forgotten is simple primary school science. Climate always changes. It is always…warming or cooling; it's never stable. And if it were stable, it would be interesting scientifically because it would be the first time in four and a half billion years." —Philip Stott, emeritus professor of biogeography at the University of London.

2006 - "Since 1895, the media has alternated between global cooling and warming scares during four separate and sometimes overlapping periods. From 1895 until the 1930's, the media peddled a coming ice age. From the late 1920s until the 1960s, they warned of global warming. From the 1950s until the 1970s, they warned us again of a coming ice age. This makes modern global warming the fourth estate's fourth attempt to promote opposing climate change fears during the last 100 years." –Senator James Inhofe, Monday, September 25, 2006.

2007- "I gave a talk recently (on fallacies of global warming), and three members of the Canadian government, the environmental cabinet, came up afterward and said, 'We agree with you, but it's not worth our jobs to say anything.' So, what's being created is a huge industry with billions of dollars of government money and people's jobs dependent on it." – Dr. Tim Ball, Coast-to-Coast, Feb 6, 2007.

2008 – "Hansen was never muzzled even though he violated NASA's official agency position on climate forecasting (i.e., we did not know enough to forecast climate change or mankind's effect on it). Hansen thus embarrassed NASA by coming out with his claims of global warming in 1988 in his testimony before Congress" – Dr. John S. Theon, retired Chief of the Climate Processes Research Program at NASA, see above for Hansen quotes. (60)

I feel that we need our fossil fuels. They are essential to our survival, at least for now. Please don't take me wrong in this volume. I am all for cleaning up our environment. I hope it will become feasible to eliminate pollution (not CO2) and switch to more practical energy means, but cutting people off from fossil fuels will be disastrous. Let's all work together to clean up the earth, but not push scare tactics that have no plausible evidence to back up some of their more ridiculous claims and predictions.

8

George Carlin: Alarmist or Denier?

Radical comedian George Carlin has an excellent bit on Climate Change. But first, let's discover who Carlin is for those who might not know.

Wikipedia: George Denis Patrick Carlin, born on May 12, 1937, and passed away on June 22, 2008, was an American stand-up comedian, social critic, actor, and author. He was regarded as one of the most important and influential stand-up comedians of all time and was dubbed "*the dean of counterculture comedians.*" He was known for his dark comedy and reflections on politics, the English language, psychology, religion, and taboo subjects.

I always enjoyed the fact that Carlin would criticize both liberal ideas and conservative ideas; he wasn't afraid to push buttons on the left or the right.

Carlin was a frequent performer and guest host on The Tonight Show during the three-decade Johnny Carson era and hosted the first episode of Saturday Night Live in 1975. The first of Carlin's 14 stand-up comedy specials for HBO was filmed in 1977 and broadcast as George Carlin at USC. From the late 1980s onwards, his routines focused on sociocultural criticism of American society. He often commented on American political issues and satirized American culture. His "seven dirty words" routine was central to the 1978 United States Supreme Court case F.C.C. v. Pacifica Foundation, in which a 5–4 decision affirmed the government's power to censor indecent material on public airwaves.

Carlin released his first solo album, Take-Offs and Put-Ons, in 1966. He went on to receive five Grammy Awards for Best Comedy Album, winning for FM & AM (1972), Jammin' in New York (1992), Brain Droppings (2001), Napalm & Silly Putty (2002), and It's Bad for Ya (2008). The latter was his final comedy special, which was filmed less than four months before his death from cardiac failure.

Carlin co-created and starred in the Fox sitcom The George Carlin Show (1994–1995). He is also known for his film performances in Car Wash (1976), Outrageous Fortune (1987), Bill & Ted's Excellent Adventure (1989), Bill & Ted's Bogus Journey (1991), The Prince of Tides (1991), Dogma (1999), Jay and Silent Bob Strike Back (2001), Scary Movie 3 (2003), and Jersey Girl (2004). He also had voice roles as Zugor in Tarzan II, Fillmore in Cars (2006), and as Mr. Conductor on Shining Time Station, as well as narrating the American dubs of Thomas & Friends.

Carlin was posthumously awarded the Mark Twain Prize for American Humor in 2008. In 2004, he placed second on Comedy Central's list of the top 10 American comedians. In 2017, Rolling Stone magazine ranked him second on its list of the 50 best stand-up comedians ever, behind Richard Pryor.

In 1959, Carlin met Jack Burns, a fellow DJ at radio station KXOL in Fort Worth, Texas. They formed a comedy team, and after successful performances at Fort Worth's beat coffeehouse called The Cellar, Burns and Carlin headed for California in February 1960.

Within weeks of arriving in California, Burns and Carlin put together an audition tape and created The Wright Brothers, a morning show on KDAY in Hollywood. While at KDAY, they honed their material in beatnik coffeehouses at night. Years later, when he was honored with a star on the Hollywood Walk of Fame, Carlin requested that it be placed in front of the KDAY studios near the corner of Sunset Boulevard and Vine Street. Burns and Carlin recorded their only album, Burns and Carlin, at the Playboy Club Tonight in May 1960 at Cosmo Alley in Hollywood. After two years as a team, they parted to pursue individual careers but "remain[ed] the best of friends."

In the 1960s, Carlin began appearing on television variety shows, where he played various characters, including a Native American sergeant, a stupid radio disc jockey, and a hippie weatherman. Variations of these routines appear on Carlin's 1967 debut album, Take-Offs and Put-Ons, recorded live in 1966 at The Roostertail in Detroit, Michigan, and issued by RCA Victor in 1967.

During this period, Carlin became a frequent performer and guest host on The Tonight Show, initially with Jack Paar as host and then with Johnny Carson. During the host's three-decade reign, Carlin became one of Carson's most frequent substitutes.

Carlin was also cast in A Way We Go, a 1967 comedy show on CBS. His early career material and appearance, which consisted of suits and short-cropped hair, had been seen as "conventional," particularly when contrasted with his later anti-establishment material.

Carlin was present at Lenny Bruce's arrest for obscenity at the Gate of Horn club in Chicago, Illinois, on December 5, 1962. As the police began detaining audience members for questioning, they asked Carlin for his identification. After responding that he did not believe in government-issued IDs, Carlin was arrested and taken to jail with Bruce in the exact vehicle.

In 1970, record producer Monte Kay formed the Little David Records subsidiary of Atlantic Records, with comedian Flip Wilson as co-owner. Kay and Wilson signed Carlin away from RCA Records and recorded a Carlin performance at Washington, D.C.'s Cellar Door in May 1971, which was released as the album FM & AM in January 1972. De Blasio was busy managing the fast-paced career of Freddie Prinze and was about to sign Richard Pryor, so he released Carlin to Little David general manager Jack Lewis, who, like Carlin, was somewhat wild and rebellious. Using his persona as a springboard for his new comedy, he was presented by Ed Sullivan in a performance of "The Hair Piece" and quickly regained his popularity as the public caught on to his sense of style.

Carlin did his skit on the climate, which you can find in its entirety on YouTube, Jamming In New York (1992)

"Everybody's gonna save something now: "Save the trees! Save the bees! Save the whales! Save those snails!" and the greatest arrogance of all: "Save the planet!" What?! Are these (expletive deleted) people kidding me?! Save the planet?! We don't even know how to take care of ourselves yet!" – Right away, we see Carlin confronting the environmentalists and their arrogance. You can tell by now that Carlin is squarely in the Denier category!

*"I'm tired of these self-righteous environmentalists; these **white, bourgeois liberals** who think the only thing wrong with this country is there aren't enough bicycle paths! People are trying to make the world safe for their Volvos! Besides, environmentalists don't give a (expletive deleted) about the planet. They don't care about the planet; not in the abstract they don't. You know what they're interested in? A clean place to live, their own habitat. They're worried that someday in the future, they might be personally inconvenienced. Narrow, unenlightened self-interest doesn't impress me."* – Carlin has occasionally attacked certain conservative viewpoints, but he wasn't afraid to attack liberal points of view either. I liked Carlin; he said what he felt and didn't care what kind of flack he got from it. *"**White Bourgeois liberals**."* Could he be talking about Al Gore? Lol.

"Besides, there is nothing wrong with the planet… nothing wrong with the planet. The planet is fine… the people are (expletive deleted)! Difference! The planet is fine! Compared to the people, THE PLANET IS DOING GREAT: Been here four and a half billion years! Do you ever think about the arithmetic? The planet has been here four and a half billion years, we've been here what? 100,000?

Maybe 200,000? And we've only been engaged in heavy industry for a little over 200 years. 200 years versus four and a half billion and we have the conceit to think that somehow, we're a threat? That somehow, we're going to put in jeopardy this beautiful little blue-green ball that's just a-floatin' around the sun?" – The Earth has been here far longer than any of us can imagine. She is the one who developed conditions that saw to our creation from a higher source. Well, that can be debated until we're blue in the face. The fact is that the planet somehow, in some way, brought us forth. Be it from nature, God, or whatever deity exists.

"The planet will be here for a long, long, LONG time after we're gone and it will heal itself, it will cleanse itself cause that's what it does. It's a self-correcting system. The air and the water will recover, the earth will be renewed, and if it's true that plastic is not degradable, well, the planet will simply incorporate plastic into a new paradigm: The Earth plus Plastic. The Earth doesn't share our prejudice towards plastic. Plastic came out of the Earth! The Earth probably sees plastic as just another one of its children." – Everything we create is based on what came from this world. Carbon emissions from fossil fuels originate from this world. Let's seek other energy sources, but not for any of the climate alarmists' reasoning. The fact is that someday, long after we're gone, fossil fuels will dry up and be no more, so what will we do?

That was a brief look at George Carlin's bit on climate; again, you can watch it on YouTube, and I highly recommend that you do.

8

Tony Heller Vs. Mallen Baker

I will summarize this volume by examining several alarmists and their ideas and contrasting them with several deniers. Instead, I will discuss two commentators: Mallen Baker, who would be closer to an alarmist, and Tony Heller, who is closer to a denier.

One of my favorite commentators on YouTube who discusses the whole climate debate is Tony Heller. He explains why he believes the way he does is based on historical records and scientific methods, both what is used today and what was used back then, and he provides documented evidence.

Tony, to be expected, has his critics, the most prominent of whom is a journalist named Mallen Baker. One of the more amusing exchanges is a series of videos in which both comments on one another. I would love to see these two in a debate, and if I had the financial resources, I would fund such a debate. But let's look at what they have to say about each other.

One area both commentators discuss concerns two graphs demonstrating an upward trend in rising temperatures. The shorter graph with red bars shows the heat wave season in the measurement of days. It began in 1960 and went into the 2010s.

The other graph went back further and showed that the 1930s were much hotter than the following decades. Tony claims that the more extended graph didn't go out to the journalists and politicians. The argument is that the temperature change wasn't linear but cyclical.

Then, the two commentators accused each other of the old bait-and-switch. Heller rightly pointed out Baker's demonstration graph was not his original one. Baker responded that it may not have been the right graph, but it shows the same thing. Then Baker showed where Tony said that himself on another website.

Another point of contention dealt with semantics. When discussing the Dust Bowl era, Baker implied that farmers contributed to the situation with improper knowledge and tools used at the time. Heller's rebuttal implied that Baker said that farmers caused the Dust Bowl situation of the 1930s, to which Baker accused Heller of pulling the old bait and switch. Baker noted that farmers contributed to the problem that day, which was a big difference.

Other videos discuss the Petermann Glacier in Greenland. The videos discuss a scientist who changed from a skeptic to an alarmist because of this glacier. Heller demonstrated that the glacier had been growing since 2012. Baker accused Heller of stating that the glacier had been advancing long-term. Heller said that Baker was using a strawman argument. He didn't tell the glacier was advancing long-term at all.

Heller then goes on to show that in 1939, all glaciers were on the verge of collapsing. He then points to an article showing the Jakobshavin glacier was rapidly retreating between 1850 and 2007. Heller then points out that the glacier had also been growing back (my comment: this happened despite the rise in CO2 emissions.) in a reversal since 2007. He then shows that the Arctic Ocean was ice-free during the time of Stonehenge. Of course, the Arctic and the Antarctic are now covered in ice despite the dramatic rise in CO2 emissions (my comment: including those caused by man in the past 200 years or more.)

Another point of contention is how Heller and Baker quote certain scientists and researchers. Heller says that Baker points out in his videos that "professional scientists said this, or professional scientists said that." While Baker counters that he never said "professional scientists," He has used the term, "researchers said."

Both cite what they believe about Milankovitch Cycles with the causes of the ice age cycles, which show the earth's orbit around the sun. It also shows that the Earth has a 23-degree tilt to its axis. The earth's orbit is elliptical, not circular, which affects our world's climate. That's why we get a short, mild winter and a long, mild summer. In ten thousand years, that will change, and we'll get short, hot summers and long, cold winters based on the earth's rotation around the sun, not CO2 emissions.

It is essential to explain that climate change and subsequent periods of glaciation, resulting from the following three variables, are not due to the total amount of solar energy reaching Earth. The three Milankovitch Cycles impact the seasonality and location of solar energy around the earth, thus impacting contrasts between the seasons. (From the Indiana University website.)

Tony disputes Baker's statement that insulation contributes to the glacial ages. Baker's researchers say that (the total Insulation received by earth has varied by <0.7 W m-2 over the past 160 kyr.) Heller believes this to be junk science. Quoting the Indiana University website, it says that it...<u>is not due to the total amount of solar energy reaching Earth</u>.

The two debate Al Gore's relevance. Baker insists that he has always been critical of Gore, but Heller says there was no severe criticism of Gore when he was receiving the Nobel Peace Prize, which is when it should have been.

Baker claims that it was just as wrong for Gore to state in his film An Inconvenient Truth that CO2 always leads to temperature changes, and it's just as bad for Tony (Heller) to imply that CO2 always follows temperature changes. Baker quotes from a research paper on the subject.

Heller responds that the paper that Baker is using to justify his claims (63) is a controversial one. I decided to look up the foremost scientist attached to this paper, **Jeremy D. Shakun**. The main criticisms of his work can be found on the website WUWT (What's Up with That?), where you can type his name in their search engine. I won't go into everything here because I'm unsure what they discuss. Like I said, I'm not a scientist, and some of the formulas they discuss go way over my head.

Heller's basic gist of the paper presented by Baker was that Shakun was almost certainly wrong, but the real issue is climate sensitivity. A change in carbon dioxide concentration can't cause a swing in temperature as large as occurs during the ice age. It's not even close.

Baker criticizes Heller's graph, which shows the fluctuation of temperatures in the Antarctic rather than globally. Heller accepts his criticism but claims it's irrelevant. He then shows the graph, which describes the fluctuation globally.

We could go on forever, but I've covered the primary source of discrepancies I wanted to show, so I'll leave you their YouTube channels in the notes section. You can review their back-and-forth criticisms and see which ones work for you. (64)

I want to mention another series on YouTube that I've grown fond of. Their work is discussed briefly in this volume: Dr. John Robson and the Climate Discussion Nexus. These shows are more professionally produced than Tony Heller's, with music and guest speakers (65). Look for all these commentators on *Facebook, Twitter,* and other social media.

I viewed many more shows on YouTube in preparation for this volume, including both the pros and cons of the climate crisis. But they were long-winded and boring, so I didn't think most of you would read every little description or detail. I fell asleep a few times myself. Therefore, I present you with the most concise of these shows. I haven't seen Al Gore's sequel to *An*

Inconvenient Truth, Spaceballs 2, the Search for More Money, I'm just kidding; it's called *Truth to Power.*

But I think I'll end this volume here. I've discussed the topics I wanted to discuss. I have more, but I'll save them for my sequel.

I doubt I'll write anything more on this topic. I've looked at how the climate alarmists change their tune with every climate change, how the 1970s "experts" scared us with *global cooling*, but when that didn't happen, they changed their tune in the 1980s to *global warming*.

We've looked at how predictions made by these "experts" failed to pass; they were made to scare the public and sell news stories. Now that temperatures aren't as hot as in the 1980s, it's being called *climate change*, which is ridiculous since the climate constantly changes. They've finally settled on the term *climate crisis*, which will change again within ten years.

Check out Kevin Given's YouTube channel and his video based on this book!

Ski resorts will have to close due to a lack of snow...NOT!

The Arctic Circle will have ice-free summers by 2017...NOT!

Notes:

1)https://en.wikipedia.org/wiki/World_Turtl
e
2) https://en.wikipedia.org/wiki/Big_Bang
3) https://www.quora.com/What-is-the-
percentage-of-CO2-in-the-atmosphere
(4)https://en.wikipedia.org/wiki/1936_North
_American_heat_wave
(5) https://en.wikipedia.org/wiki/Dust_Bowl
(6)https://wattsupwiththat.com/2013/03/01/
global-cooling-compilation/
7) Sumter Daily Item - January 26, 1970
8) St. Petersburg Times - Mar 4, 1970
9) The Day - Nov 1, 1971
10) Eugene Register-Guard - May 29, 1974
11) New York Times - January 5, 1978
12) St. Petersburg Times - June 26, 1970
13) The Bryan Times March 31 - 1973
14) Boca Raton News – January 17, 1978
15) New York Times - May 21, 1978
16) Newsweek - April 28, 1975
17) The Robesonian – March 3, 1975
18) The Free Lance-Star – September 11, 1972
19)https://en.wikipedia.org/wiki/Snow_in_F
lorida
20) James Hansen's testimony before
Congress in June 1988

21) San Jose Mercury News 1986
22) "Global Warming Has Begun." New York Times, June 24, 1988.
23) AP PETER JAMES SPIELMANN June 29, 1989
24) The Independent - September 15, 2014
25) New Scientist – April 7, 2007
26) BBC News – December 12, 2007
27) Daily Caller – June 19, 2018
28) https://en.wikipedia.org/wiki/Polar_bear
29) http://whslionspride.com/2017/06/polar-bears-are-going-extinct-and-that-has-to-stop/
30) https://www.worldwildlife.org/species/polar-bear
31) https://polarbearfacts.net/why-are-polar-bears-going-extinct/
32) https://www.polarbear-world.com/polar-bear-endangered/
33) https://grist.org/article/will-polar-bears-go-extinct-by-2030-part-i/
34) https://fee.org/articles/the-myth-that-the-polar-bear-population-is-declining/
35) https://arcticwwf.org/species/polar-bear/population/
36) https://www.ibtimes.com/polar-bear-population-higher-20th-century-something-fishy-about-extinction-fears-821075
37) https://www.youtube.com/watch?v=8ZUoYGAI5i0

38)https://wattsupwiththat.com/2011/11/22/ al-gores-global-warming-claims-on-kilimanjaro-glacier-finally-dead-and-buried-in-the-climategate-2-0-emails-even-phil-jones-and-lonnie-thompson-dont-believe-it/
39) https://cei.org/pdf/5539.pdf
40) https://skepticalscience.com/co2-temperature-correlation.htm
41) The Courier-Mail; Monday 6 May 1940
42)https://notalotofpeopleknowthat.wordpress.com/2019/06/20/ice-melting-in-greenland-thats-what-it-does-in-summer/
43) http://nsidc.org/greenland-today/2013/02/greenland-melting-2012-in-review/
44) https://youtu.be/ewJ6TI8ccAw
45)https://en.wikipedia.org/wiki/Naomi_Oreskes
46)https://www.forbes.com/sites/larrybell/2012/07/17/that-scientific-global-warming-consensus-not/#4869f43b3bb3
47)https://en.wikipedia.org/wiki/Surveys_of_scientists%27_views_on_climate_change
48)https://journals.ametsoc.org/na101/home/literatum/publisher/ams/journals/content/bams/2014/15200477-95.7/bams-d-13-00091.1/20140821/images/large/i1520-0477-95-7-1029-t01.jpeg
49)https://en.wikipedia.org/wiki/James_Hansen

50) The Canberra Times – Monday September 26, 1988

51) National Post – Wednesday October 21st, 2009

52)https://notalotofpeopleknowthat.wordpress.com/2018/06/22/the-failed-predictions-of-james-hansen/

53)https://www.pbs.org/wgbh/pages/frontline/hotpolitics/interviews/wirth.html

54) https://principia-scientific.org/studies-arctic-sea-ice-increasing-since-the-1930s/

55) https://principia-scientific.org/studies-arctic-sea-ice-increasing-since-the-1930s/

56) The Canberra Times – Thursday July 18, 1963

57)https://www.climatecentral.org/library/faqs/plants_need_co2_to_live_so_isnt_more_of_it_a_good_thing

58)https://en.wikipedia.org/wiki/Greta_Thunberg

59)https://en.wikipedia.org/wiki/2019_UN_Climate_Action_Summit

60)https://710wor.iheart.com/featured/mark-simone/content/2019-10-08-the-list-of-120-years-of-climate-scares-by-scientists/

61)

62)
https://www.nytimes.com/2018/07/19/climate/climate-lawsuit-new-york.html

63) https://www2.bc.edu/jeremy-shakun/Shakun%20et%20al.,%202012,%20Nature.pdf

64)
https://www.youtube.com/user/TonyHeller1
https://www.youtube.com/channel/UCZrXbiKCUkRNdoDgn3sDXqw

65)
https://www.youtube.com/channel/UC_egdS4871949youPFyvW_A

Bibliography

<u>The New Ice Age by Henry Gilfond</u>
Published by Watts in New York, ISBN
0531014584

**<u>The weather conspiracy: the coming of
the new ice age: a report</u>** Publisher:
Ballantine Books ISBN 0345272099

**<u>Blizzard What Happens If It Doesn't
Stop? by George Stone</u>** Publisher: Grosset
& Dunlap ASIN: B000HZJOTG

**<u>The Cooling: Has the Next Ice Age
Already Begun? by Lowell Ponte</u>**
Publisher: Roadblaster1 ISBN 013172312X

**<u>Cool IT (Movie Tie-in Edition): The
Skeptical Environmentalist's Guide to
Global Warming by Bjorn Lomborg</u>**
Vintage; Media Tie In edition ISBN:
9780307741103

<u>I Am Not Spock – by Leonard Nimoy</u>
Publisher: Celestial Arts ISBN: 0890871175

I Am Spock – by Leonard Nimoy
Publisher: Hachette Books ISBN-10: 0316388378

The Climate Wars: How the Consensus is Enforced - by Brandon Shollenberger
Publisher: Amazon ASIN: B01CEZLAM0

Climate, History and The Modern World – H. H. Lamb Publisher: Routledge; 2 edition (August 17, 1995) ISBN 9780415127356

Inconvenient Facts: The Science That Al Gore doesn't want you to know by Gregory Wrightstone Publisher: Silver Crown ISBN: 1545614105

The Politically Incorrect Guide to Climate Change (The Politically Incorrect Guides) by Marc Morano Publisher: Regnery Publishing ISBN1621576760

God And the Astronomers by Robert Jastrow Publisher: Norton ISBN-0393011879